components of a semi-functional human being

Components of a Semi-Functional Human Being by Megan Munson

Cover and illustrations by Kim Kazanowski.

for anyone who's just stoked to be here

TABLE OF CONTENTS

I: CARBON

II: MARROW

III: MUD

I: CARBON

highline

she kind of looked like god
when she told me Not to drink the bitch cup
i'd just shot into in that low-ceilinged basement;
perhaps my vision was blurred
as i wore those goggles of
Too Much Smirnoff,
but that heavenly glint in her eyes
turned me sober.

i've never been a fan of
omniscience
but she riddled it with mystery.
over a glass of cheap
merlot she told me that
she knew me Wholly,
but i'd never live to see the day
she felt like understanding.

i found myself in a pew
grasping a bottle of
Barefoot.

she helped me untie my shoes
took off my Keystone-drenched socks
and watched as i began to walk
this sober highline.
i'm calling upon the apes we evolved
from, but my balance disappeared
somewhere along that cladogram
like a tail or the need for
an appendix.
she shouts encouragement and i'm
drawn across this line
as i feel these instinctual wants bubble up
inside of me like the light carbonation
of a Montucky Cold Snack.

my toes are beginning to freeze and i wish
we hadn't lost that neanderthal covering.
she sounds like going back in time;
a delorean ride to when my lips didn't
taste like rubbing alcohol.
she has me considering creationism
and craving communion wine.
everything feels vestigial except for
her.

thank you for the sunbeams

i don't know you, golden boy
but you are among the trees when autumn erupts across the city
and glistening in winter's highest peak

you are more than i could know
and when you whisper through your warmth
you are august defined

laced with sunlight, tied with grace
i could sunbathe in your laughter
lie with me until the rain passes

i will never deserve to have danced with the sun,
but i hope to god that these tan lines remain
crossed along my darkened shoulders like scars;
a fleeting attempt to capture
your golden sheen.

a stuttering heart's protest of love poems

i've trapped the sun in my pillowcase
cotton and soft duvet, we skip the top sheet
and burrow

i listen to the valves of your heart
       open, shut
           open, shut
                open, shut
like a screen door battling the wind

you built a home in your lungs
and i dozed off on the doorstep.
take care to leave the porch light on.

quiet wants, quieter sunrises

unfound is the romance of dawn
and i cannot wait for it to be discovered

let's find solace in soggy tofu scramble and oversteeped tea,
open the windows wide and invite the day to breakfast
understand how our 6:30 alarms mimic the birds
and that the day begins only once the coffee's been poured

we'll meet mornings with drowsy eyes and timid smiles
and each day,
perhaps i'll be lucky enough
to wake alongside the sun.

i grew you a garden

i grew you a garden.
i loved the way my palms were coated in more mud than skin
even as the soil sullied my cheekbones.
blood moved through my arteries like phloem sap.
i found shade beneath the sunflowers
and purpose in the peonies.

you simply nodded when i showed you.

i guess it's pretty

as the earth built essence beneath your feet and bestowed upon me the
privilege of fostering her leaved children she held my hands through her
wettened soil and kept me warm in her providing rains constantly preg-
nant and birthing the life that stood taller than our meager shoulders
More Than Merely Pretty

i shouted

THIS WAS ALL FOR YOU

but already those vines i so tenderly raised
had shot through your ear canals
and rendered you unhearing.
in a month's time, flowers will bloom in your cerebellum.

i am sorry for the way my plants claimed your body
how these petals so quickly covered your pupils
and put you to sleep as imposter eyelids.
i am sorry you could not see why this is right.
already you sink into the soil as though it's tempur pedic,
blessed to be fertilizer.

i'll lay beside you and wait to be held
knowing now how your bloodless hands will never warm me
like the sun's rays
knowing now that i can only find home in this earth.

to weathermen

i spent long enough beneath the cloud cover to never see the sun
and when it shone through stratus,
i was told not to stare
then came september's bright skies
parasols and sunglasses were tossed aside
and i looked up

i've been a loyal follower of the rain.
i find comfort in the way it flows down the living room window panes
ricochets off the back tires of fast-moving cars
and washes you of the week if you're lucky enough to be caught in it

but the sun never left me shivering;
it kissed my shoulders, never scorching
said gentle goodnights and good mornings
left me with sunspots and memories

i still long for the rain come a too-hot dry spell,
but for now, i'll dance in the sunbeams
let them warm my shoulders to tenderness
darken and freckle my cheeks
and hold gently
the backs of my arms.

beating, battling

i'm quarrelling with my heart
as it beats too hard for comfort.
it's speaking a language half-forgotten,
like the one you took for a semester in high school
before donating all of those english-translation dictionaries.

there's no duolingo for the soul,
so i'll speak in pidgin until my BPM lowers,
mutter something along the lines of
Hey I Thought We Weren't Doing This Anymore —
Can You Settle Down Over There?

the sentiment is lost in translation.

soon, i'm sure,
our conversation will simmer to a monologue
as that pulsing organ speaks for me;
i can only play devil's advocate for so long —
i don't need to be fluent
to see that it knows best.

a lack of priorities, a lack of oxygen

maybe yellowstone will take us in an ashy arc
or maybe someone will build jurassic park
we'll be trampled by a t-rex or, on another sci-fi thread,
maybe aliens will show up and we'll all end up dead
i wouldn't mind being forced to go to the stars
i'd go anywhere as long as i am where you are
but i wonder if maybe that won't be the case —
if the end will be born of a better-known place
like disease that rots us all from inside
and i'll lay by you till my organs have died
is it romantic to share a last breath?
to live life together and then to meet death
as a duo? a team?
i can't say it seems
like the plot of a film
i'd pay money to see
but i'd watch you all day as the comets came down
wouldn't even look up, just would stare as you frown
and mention earth science, say this doesn't make sense
until god himself had cut you off mid-sentence
i'll watch it occur, as earth turns overdue
as even her terminal blast fails to outshine you.

droughts and dousings

we straightened our elbows to reach for constellations
and you told me how it felt to be golden.
i suddenly noticed the drought that had reached my root tips.

i could not compete with the bonfire.
limitlessly, it reached for the sky
until its smoky clouds blocked out the planets i'd held so dearly to.
i longed to retreat into the blackness
but my ankles remained tangled in the earth.

blackberry brambles hugged the tops of our feet
like shoelaces tied too tight.
they reddened our wintered skin as the flames licked higher
as we lost sight of the space beyond.

summer held you close

you are bathed in sunset orange
i, beside you
and there is grit beneath my fingernails
and sweat across my brow
and clarity in my heart.
i know the freckles
that dash your shoulders;
how the sun greets your pale skin each summer
and leaves you kissed until mid-january.
you smile and the sun rises again
as though the winter solstice has ended.
painted with similarities, we live colorblind
and i long for the sun to kiss me, too.

(but winter sent you shivering)

in it crept like a bitterness on the tongue
six p.m.'s golden caress
a fine pairing of sunset and the wind's bite

there was the grit beneath fingernails.
there was the spattering of freckles on shoulders.
there was the sun's blinding reflection.

like the wind's breath it passed over
and was not tasted again.

bad tenants

i have a good friend who lives in the back of my brain
who goes by the name of self-doubt.
i hadn't meant to rent out that room
(and i certainly don't remember him signing a lease)
but he's settled in to the extent that i can't rightly evict him.

my tenant is quiet
but makes himself remembered when he wants to.
for instance,
he called the landlord almost instantly
when you kissed me on that park bench.

he buzzed himself in
said "how platonic!"
and excused himself only after a matter of hours
of sitting on my couch
eating the produce i had reserved for dinner
and drinking me dry of earl grey.

i wish he hadn't let himself in —
my mental rows of apartments are at capacity
and love is asking to co-sign with friendship and desire.
i'd call for help,
 but this unwanted guest seems to have taken up the room
that security had once inhabited.

i hope he'll leave with time
(or at least make rent this month).

atomic

i want to be the molecules
you exhale when you're thinking hard or maybe
the skin cells caught on the edge of your cheek
i want to be microscopic and plentiful
carried on the breeze through your hair
i want to be anything but as big
as i feel today i need to
shrink so i can fit in your arms
so you can interlace your fingers
with my ribcage
so i can
again again again
put my flimsy decrepit self
into the hands of someone seemingly more
capable.

used to

i used to love you.
i did it most when you let the sun in
it slipped through your sieve of a smile
you let the wind breathe through those pores
timid chiming of a mid-spring birds' nest
your words felt like mud beneath my feet
so i let them slide between my toes and dirty my soles
until they froze in that watery muck
shivered in that flooded meadow.

i used to love you
when you took to the wind like a lightless leaf
left me rooted and wondering if the breeze would return you
if i would again be adorned by that viridescent jacket
i longed for that corset of a canopy
did not recognize the beauty of my own bark
bent my cellulose backbone
curved my spine to match the willow.

i used to love you
like a leech loves plasma and platelets
i turned vampire against your skin
affixed my canines and wandered from my roots
your heart's cocktail felt different on my teeth
so i let that new flavor infiltrate my mouth
swished it around like an unfamiliar merlot
let you stain my molars and sully my esophagus
ignored how your blood tasted of bitter aluminum
felt bile mumble in my gut
ignored that groaning protest
rejected the cry of my chemoreceptors and chose instead
to swallow.

i used to love you
even though you told me i felt like the sea;
not her beautiful enormity but her swells,
her typhoons and drownings
her vicious undertow.

i used to love you
because you replaced the sun with your light
artificial 30-watt LED imposter of the beams on my skin
blinding, cooling
did not let me grow.

i used to love you
as you built us into a home of brick and mortar
and neglected to leave space for a window.

i used to love you
more than i loved the world because
the world was something
you did not let me know.

thunderstorms

i always thought storms were built for two.

i thought maybe we would lay outside
and count lightning and thunder.
i can't remember which precedes which,
but i'm sure somehow, you'd know.
we'd do arithmetic until we caught those bolts in our hands
until they illuminated our Wettened smiling faces
even better than the sun could.

or maybe we'd seek shelter from that rain,
try to preserve our warmth until
that skysea soaked our scalps
and the atmosphere boomed that no umbrella
could match her downpour.
we'd learn to dance in it instead.

my favorite part is always the thunderclap —
that cumulonimbus shout across the sky
rattling my brick shelter and reminding me that the heavens
could anytime overtake my ceiling.
i think perhaps you favored the lightning
those blinding, singular flashes
gone before their thunderous counterpart
has a chance to say goodbye.

i'm learning how to watch storms for two.
i'm laying in this late-spring mud and trying to catch
as many falling drops as i can.
i'll bask in these watery beams
until those asphalt clouds quit their beautiful tantrums
until they leave me drenched and alone beneath an empty sky.

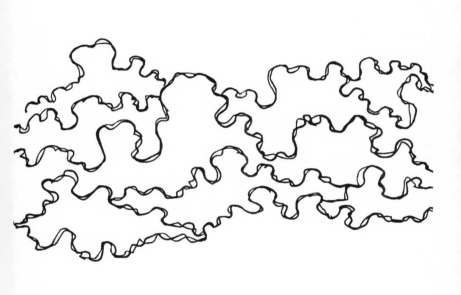

tell me again

tell me again how sea monsters are your hometown heroes
i see you only in dry spells and sand
and those who laugh less often than they should
i am afraid of the ocean so i do not meet your eyes do not
allow myself to fall into typhoon pupils i know too well
how my lungs beg for collapse come the tidal wave
skinny comes home to your shoulderblades
your slight self tell me again
about the hum of your engine
how it quiets beneath the river's roar i
have never wanted so desperately to drown
i met the mountains and they untaught me how to swim
so catch me swallowed by the sea
uh-oh. have i contradicted myself?
i've leapt headfirst off the peak i promised
i wouldn't climb again but the waters called me back
you called me back so i'll call you
home tell me again what you last muttered under your breath
i didn't catch it over the sound of three gallons
filling my eardrums i didn't catch it over
the tsunami you met me with
you told me it was home and now my socks are wet
and i am uncomplaining tell me again
how my shoes will dry on the hearth after you've left

i don't want them to.

i'll take my bony ankles sopping back to the rockies
i'll walk until they crack wetly beneath my savage enormity
i wish i could float like you tell me again
how it feels to be buoyant how it feels
to lose yourself even during low tide
god, is that what the cigarettes granted you?
i wonder how my lungs would fare if i traded mountain air
for your dewy brine crashing and weightless and home
you wrote these oceans i see your sloppy penmanship
in the whirl of the waves and wonder
how any cartographer managed to find their way
through your abysmal works tell me again
how poseidon's trident is a ballpoint pen
and you see him in a still pool's reflection
tell me again when you learned to breathe underwater
how perhaps i could too
tell me again as you hold my head beneath the surface
and take me home.

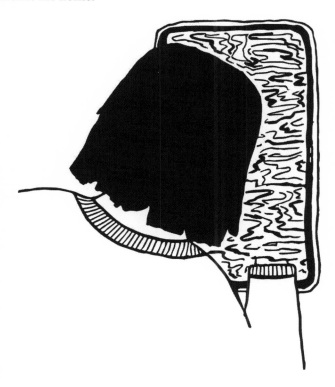

how much is airfare today?

the space just to my right has felt a little empty lately
as though i've been accompanied by a ghost
who just recently up and left

i grew tired of that excess air
so i shoved my bed against the wall
and pretended there wasn't even room for two

i've started piling things in my passenger seat
to disguise it as something full
pretending that rush-hour commutes are just as fun alone

i'm adapting to sitting in the middle of the couch
and waiting for movies to arrive on Netflix
rather than paying for a suddenly too-large theater seat

i've stopped going out for dinner
because a table for two
is now a whole size too big

i am filling the cavity to my right with anything i can find
burning time and warming my fingers over the bonfire
remembering how to be alone and yearning
for the new year.

time's trap and pendulum

tick, tock
echoes in her sternum and cochlea alike
sun sets those beams of   light drip down her corneas like a
broken   faucet
          sting like   lemon juice
stained lens to retina tick, tock
          say those years and she remembers that
she's seen this light before
that her scleras are stained like books left in the sun too long
she'd   crack them open but she's read them time and again already
it has been years
          since she has known anything but   tick, tock
yellow
she blinks.   she blinks.   she   blinks.
lemon acid burns she does not realize what
          she tick, tock does not see;
that acid seeps into her rod cells tick,
          tock everything is going black
she has been here before. she has been here before. she has been here
          for years and she refuses to leave feels   that tick, tock
glass capsule like a hug it's the
          one-way   mirror
of a Criminal Minds rerun and she sees not
tick, tock   the world outside she does tick, tock not
          know how her pocket watch hangs in
the starry night now that the sun has set swings
tick, tock across the cosmos
          she stares instead at
the face the face the porcelain tick t i c k tick   face
wonders not even of the   TOCK gears that turn behind it
tick, tock knows only those three hands wants only to see them
          Repeat Repeat Repeat
past those   tick   Safe   tock   Familiar numbers
does not dream of the future.

pinterest

i've begun turning to pinterest to remind myself of things
soft. i scroll through gardens and recipes for cakes until
my eyes might bleed and i do it with the
sordid motive of resurrecting a life with you that could
have been. i tried logging out on my laptop once
and i only lasted two hours before the call of
a million vegan dinner ideas lured me back. i'll scroll
through the recipes for hours, but i always just imagine
eating them with you. same goes for the garden. pinterest
points out a way to edge the grass with little
rocks and i imagine us laying bricks into the dirt
and spending an afternoon in the lavender just like we
did last july. i would get dirt under my nails
despite the fact that i keep them short and halfway
through, you'd get inspired enough for a second trip to
Molbak's. it could be decades before our garden looked more
than half-assed, but i guess we were always misguided
by ambition. i could spend nights out there, skin muddy
and you beside me, and you would name the state's
indigenous plants and the ones that had moved in unwelcome
like white men on huge ships. and we'd laugh. we'd
laugh until the sun rose and doused our garden in
its warmth.

i watched as the lavender died. my garden is lonely and filled with weeds.
you are not here. pinterest is open in the next tab.

an official rejection of secondary colors

i'm green!
in a couple of ways but mostly in the clay that coats my face
it burns my eyes and i watch them water quickly in that circular mirror
and say oh THAT'S why you aren't supposed
to put tea tree oil near your eyes
but i feel the same burn in my fingertips and hip bones and
goddamn Trapezius Muscles
like my bones have been liquified into salicylic acid
and now dissolve my unraveling ligaments
lizard green i remember
being followed home and someone put Shrek on but i fell asleep
too warm two arms something new and familiar
and allegedly i began to snore but you can't trust
everything you hear because i look ogre-esque now
and old truths seem like fantasy
we were painted green
one night beneath lights that blink a little too quickly to sleep under
spread gunk on our faces green green
like my brother coloring in a rainforest with me
crouched on the living room floor
he took his green marker and drew in little circles
and i, clutching crayola, almost
entirely lost my shit because i color in lines
i couldn't coexist with those circular scribbles because i needed
consistency and unity and for things to be the same
but there are way too many shades of green for that to be realistic
way too many shades of everything and i miss knowing only primary
colors like the

red

that lines my eyes above my mask
burning a little, drying a little
and turning me green.

fate

i met Fate clutching
a six-pack of Angry Orchard
and singing to himself.

his voice was higher than i remembered.

"i   think
          we're   all going
to the
          Same
                    Place"

he told me
and then turned 180 degrees.

i burrowed into my bed and heard Fate laughing outside my window.
he raved about espresso as i spilled tea onto my shoes.
Fate got stuck in the elevator while i was taking the stairs.

Fate's arms were not built for holding so he stretches
past me and into his mirror he
muddles his face flexes his skin
like it's playdough pulls it taut over his bones
and then scrunches it into his cheeks
smiles fatly like an infant
tugs on his throat like he's plastic
splashes in some paint like a cartoon recolor
builds a Barbie from a boy
and now prefers IPAs.

i met Fate
shouting at a concert
watching Planet Earth
pulling an espresso shot
climbing in the Cascades
sitting in my math class

singing to himself.

II: MARROW

birdbrain

my skin is pulled tight over a wrought-iron cage
that a chickadee flew into,
lodging itself in my esophagus and shimmying down my pallid neck
landing with a thump upon my diaphragm and existing there
not to sing breath into my withering lungs
but to flutter and fly
to play my ribs like a xylophone
to quicken my heart and turn my breath feather-filled and weak
only to eventually curl up and rest
as dead weight in the cavity of my chest.

it is one thing to carry your bags on your back
or to lug them behind you in a suitcase,
but you would not believe the damage
of a few extra ounces in my chest.
i recall its last song before it slipped into my mouth
to meet flesh and feather and a lack of air.
i haven't filled my lungs in ages
my mouth tastes of decay
i do not part my lips for fear of letting that bird's last breath escape.

i hold that little puff of air beneath my tongue
and purse my chapped lips.
i can feel the weight of its light grey body at the base of my left lung.
my heart pumps harder against the weight.
my throat still aches from a long trench
left by the chickadee's beak in its descent.
i imagine how its tiny talons tried to grasp the sides of my organs;
how it punctured my alveoli in an attempt to cling to anything at all;
how it failed to hold on.

porcelain

i have always been afraid of ceramics
i worry that my hands — clumsy, too-big —
will spill porcelain onto the floor
that my feet, eager to meet one another,
will trip and i will tumble
into a field of beauty cracked and shattered.

i am not gentle enough for porcelain.
i grip my mugs with two hands
even when they burn from the water within.
i stack my plates with care because i worry
they'll chip like a left front tooth.
i don't use saucers for fear
that they'll fall apart in my palms.

i see the beauty of china
and wish that i was soft enough for it to be made for me
but i know these rough hands would scratch off the paint
these feet would stack and stumble
that softness would split and crumble
and leave me stranded
in a mass of broken white.

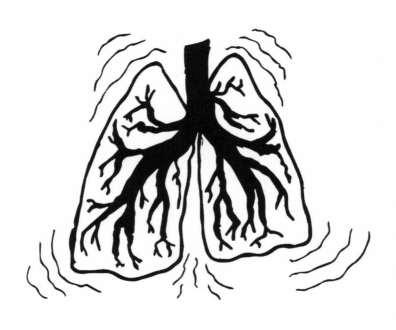

i bought a tube of panic for $2.97

have you ever hyperventilated while brushing your teeth?
it's like being waterboarded by mint
lungs held captive by colgate
torture of listerine and hysteria
a fear you can't spit into the bathroom sink.

panic feels like a broken faucet.
first, droplets of agitation meet porcelain
until the sink is full
       (second, you think of how much water you're wasting
       and just feel worse about the whole thing).

the mirror above the bathroom sink is perfectly clean
but you can't recognize yourself.
the world becomes small beyond the buzz of your electric toothbrush
until you feel it has shrunk to the size of your bathroom
and the oxygen is leaving that tiled room.

all that exists is you
and that
refreshing
minty flavor.

rush hour

my heart is in stop-and-go traffic
but my brain is going 70 across the 520 bridge
my eyelids are flirting with each other
but i refuse to let them meet
because all i can imagine are four heavy wheels skidding
on this still-wet roadway
my bones lying out on the freeway
alabaster replacements of the lines that divide one lane from another

this commute makes me ugly
because i thought i was a pacifist until 5 p.m. on a tuesday
when nearly everyone merged incorrectly and suddenly i wanted war
i'm shouting Zipper! Zipper! Zipper! but i'm not a driver's ed teacher
just a girl with a too-big car
and terrible gas mileage

i feel age as the minutes tick on
as my lower back begins to ache
and i begin to worry about things like lumbar support
i forget the freedom of the outdoors
when the cloud cover conceals rainier
making for a world of only black night and brake lights
and wanting desperately to go home.

rejects of the fruit salad

disheartening
is the bruised peach at the top of your fruit bowl
and you hadn't known how it had rolled
off of its pile at the supermarket
over the side of its box
onto the grimy floor of the produce section
or how someone had the heart to replace it
but not to take it home.
had you known the poor fruit's history
you wouldn't have chosen it either.
how unfair
(of you)
that is.

you surely will not eat it now.
not with that purplish, softening mark.
it is destined to rot.

burn the witch, water her ashes

it lands with a sizzle on already-blackening skin
as she notices april's arrival
too little too late
as the flames lick higher.
that pitter-patter is a taunt from god.
she is rooted like the trees but she will not drink
this tardy deliverance;
her throat Aches
for a reprieve but to open her mouth
would mean an invitation addressed
to that billowing smoke.
she will croak as the clouds move in
and these showers will outlive her
just long enough to extinguish
her flickering embers.

learning to swim in the rapids

it turns from enough to too much with great haste
and suddenly the kiddie pool becomes the ocean
no one had predicted such wind speeds
but the saltwater tastes like going home
the desire to be full is greater than the desire to swim
emptiness is what causes the fall
it becomes easy to sink when you already know pressure
wavetops singing
crashing
gulp, do not paddle
swallow, do not swim
that chilling tide feels like an embrace
to be known by the seas
to be adopted by Poseidon
you will know Atlantis
take to the bottom of the ocean
collapse in the sand
answer the call of the depths
not kicking
not gasping
do not paddle
do not swim
sink.

blinking billboards

i first saw her on a billboard just off a highway without rest stops.
someone had clambered up the ladder and graffitied Xes over her eyes
given her wolflike canines
woman turned predator for the sight of the
handful that drove these country roads

mother told me she was sin
preacher told me she would be my End
and i knew this as i stared at her painted-on features
at her red and deep and sorrowful
longed for her through the glass of that backseat windowpane
begged dad to slow the car so i could learn to remember
her

as he stepped on the gas i swear to heaven and hell that
those bloodred heavy-lashed full-tinted eyes winked slowly at me
dared me to leap out the back windshield
to spray that near-empty road with shards of glass and skin
to climb that ladder myself
and redeem her smiling face from the blind

i met her again years later on a saturday night
coked-up hero of an unfamiliar place this time Closer
she pulled me in as my instincts went under
dared me to sink into long black hair
i watched her pupils grow until i thought they should burst
like a lysed red blood cell
fucked-up experiment of vision and osmosis
i felt her nails too-long dog-like born of cerberus
rake my sides back neck
as she showed me that love and sin hurt the same way
she whispered in my ear and then bit it off
kissed my jaw until it unlocked
held my hands so tightly that my fingers swelled
my nails popped off one by one like a ten-second countdown
that would hurtle me into those deep-space strands
good and bad amount only to blood
i felt bile in my throat and wondered if it was love

she invited me to stay so i laid sweat-soaked in a bed i didn't recognize.
i felt her feeding me nightmares those eight hours but i woke
to an emptiness beside me
two eyes full of sleep and tears i don't remember shedding
a body bruisedbittenaching.

we made a date thirty years down the line
and i'd forgotten until she knocked on my door
apologized for Ghosting me those decades prior.

she strolled around my home as though it was her own
overtook seven sandalwood candles with that alluring perfume of rot
cast me following behind her blindly

she pretended not to see the scars she left me with
looked at my family portraits lovingly and then Spat on them
cooked a five-course meal and fed it to the basement rats

on the tile her heels clicked a little too loudly for my quiet house
she kissed me by the kitchen sink and her breath lingered in my mouth
peanut butter cling wrap of a taste unleaving

she lapped at the blood that stained my kitchen floor,
stood over me, winked,
heavyeyesbigeyesredeyesempty
returned to her billboard.

an unconcerning poem about cutlery

i have found a new piece of silverware
in a drawer i've opened every day for years
and i know that i accidentally stole it from somewhere
(probably from my favorite thai place three blocks away).
i've never condoned theft but what am i going to do?
stroll through the front doors of a restaurant and confess my sins?
i'm not one to admit my faults and everybody knows it
but they also know that i am crammed with flaws
and lessons to be learned
which is fine because i know i have a problem
but i don't have a diagnosis
so i'm stuck by the kitchen sink (fork in hand)
wondering what the sidewalk outside of that thai restaurant
would taste like
and asking when cutlery became too much for consideration
but isn't it just a fork
and am i not okay?

that problematic four-pronged utensil
disappears again beneath the countertop
as i shut the kitchen drawer.

calculus

dinnertime feels like a conference of calculus and
my porcelain plate is a midterm.
i'm trying to do arithmetic but these variables aren't adding up
why can't i learn anything beyond subtraction?
what's the limit of my capacity to relapse?
(the limit does not exist)
how many calories do i count for
swallowing the fact that i wasn't worth fighting for?

i'm suddenly less of a bookworm and more of a calculator.
i want to count every alveoli sac in my lungs
every vein that crisscrosses my forearm
every ridge in these bitten nails.
i want to make myself transparent;
erased like a homework problem so clearly incorrect
that you have to start all over again
see-through until the inventory of my body
is taken and sorted into an excel sheet

my skin is flirting with my bones again
but i'm trying to ignore the way the
two press up against each other.
(i know it would be bad for me
to move into someone right now,
so i'm not trying to promote romance
beneath my own flesh.)
i can't differentiate between blood and marrow.
i don't even know how to approach the equations
that my ribs are writing to me.
i'm in the market for a math tutor.

american

the way we fade is simple and horrible.
we leave sometimes with a stutter,
and sometimes with a shout
i cannot understand why our moments are ripped from us

                                 too soon too soon

and we echo and echo and echo until that too fades

i am so young. i am so young. i am so young.
i cannot take their departures
we know

too soon

                                 too soon too soon

they are too young. we are too young.

thoughts and prayers and thoughts and prayers and
echoes
stuck on repeat, fingers curled they will not move

      too young

left with a shout. how?
i know you not
but i hear the echo
i hear the echo
i cannot escape the echo

to grow old is to die
but to die too young is to leave

too soon

so much in so little
despite rolling on the right track on the right track
followed the rules followed the right track
straight to the hospital bed

                                 too soon

the weight of a stranger too soon collides collides
too soon and so far and unknown and too close
to be reminded that youth is not invincibility
the knowing power left my bones

                                  too soon

to be carefree to be safe to be silenced
unfair

                                  too soon
echoing

too soon
gone

                          too soon too soon too soon

unfathomable.

marathon

you have started running again
and i can't help but remember how you told me
the way you hate the heat that fills your lungs
the pressure in your knees
even the sound of your feet against the pavement.

has she crawled back inside
of your pale, protruding ribs?

i know how you dwindle
how your mass rises and falls
as you hear the scream of the scale summon you
back into your wretched ways.

some days are not meant for eating,
as you substitute liquid for lunch
          (and breakfast)
                    (and dinner)

you crave visible crevices
slicing across your shoulder blades and stomach.
you want only to see your collarbones
and to feel the weight of the world directly on your skeleton.

you have started running again.
you are losing the race.

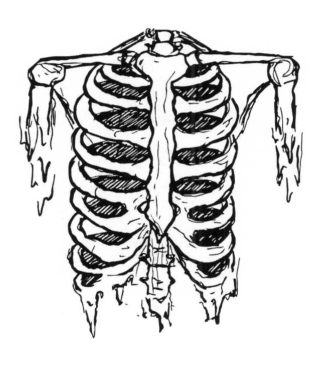

an orchard, an orchestra, picking at my skin

she played host at a depressive dinner party
as guests lined up empty-stomached and high-hoped
pulled out chairs and tied on bibs
preparing for the feast of the year.

the twelfth showed up empty-handed despite its promises.
it was far too late to hire a caterer,
so they picked at empty plates
and politely pretended to love the way hunger played its chords
in the symphonies of their ever-receding stomachs.

empty and starved and unable to say it
they sat silent as their brow bones protruded over darkening eyes
their cheeks turned concave, their necks stiffened
atop collarbones deeper than the serving platters

they could not bear orchestra's roar any longer!
its longing, repetitive tune
rang painful as it met the linings of their guts .

out to the orchard ran the twelve
(the failed provider following slowly,
caught in the burly arms of guilt).
moon's rays met flesh and bone.

it was far from the promised feast,
but they had not known food in so long
that the branches were gourmet —
roast chicken of the hungry

warped as their bodies was their concept of fullness,
and yet their hearts felt so.
they sought comfort in overripe fruit,
but the contentment of their stomachs
was not enough to be made whole.
they built their bones of cherry pits
and pretended they were as strong
as pine.

muddying my marrow. not a sprout in sight.

i wish i could feel my blood like wet soil,
could recognize that like the garden i grow dearly
i need nourishment to expand these roots
to reach towards the sun
to grow to my full potential

my bones feel like weeds and i'm trying to pull them to the surface.
i'm scraping through this groundcover in an attempt to see
what's underneath but i'm too impatient to allow time
for these sprouts to emerge from their seeds.

i feel the sun on my skin and i put up an umbrella.
others devour my crop and i let the pests in.
i will not let myself grow.

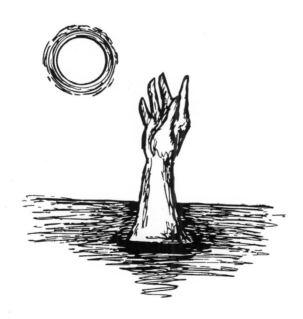

III: MUD

a wind, a bargain, a hopeful reduction of the cloud cover

there is a noisy peace
when the clouds turn lavender in october.
pastels never seem to accompany thunder,
but nature booms that she will have her way

i will sit in the downpour until we muster up a deal
"okay, sweetheart, i'll stop using k-cups
if you stop drowning my geraniums,"
i'll whisper through the storm

until she quiets her roar
until november comes
with the promise of baby-blue skies.

afternoons alongside rainier

throughout the meadow, we cry our delights:
how beautiful it can be to run through the grass!
to feel the tick's bite!
to let the mud seep in between our toes!

the grass sighs calmly a welcome;
it carries the breath of the wind
through its countless appendages.

wildflowers sharpen the image of softness.
we take care to step gently.

there is the scent of cedar in the breeze.
and the call of the crickets as they welcome us home.
how easy it is, to love without destroying.
how easy it is, not to conquer.

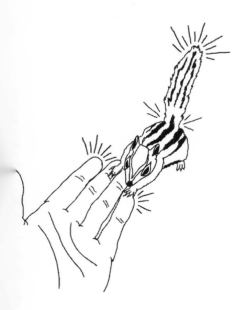

splintering granite // sturdy pine

i did not rest between breaths
for fear that my lungs would give in
at 6000 feet
while my oxygen tank sat by my
bedside table at sea level hundreds
of miles away we
kissed the sky in new mexico
but it would not kiss us back so
we kissed each other instead
in a tent built for five that
wanted nothing more than to
float towards the big dipper or to
careen itself in one starlit gust off that cliff
into our neighbor the gorge and
i can't believe i didn't do the same
after all of that spiced rum but
the rock held my hands and said "hey
this is why we moved out here and
turned roots to sediment and
abandoned the woods you know
so well" and i felt that from my sprained
ankles to the calluses on my fingertips as
though the cellulose had condensed into
8 thick places on my hands where
the rock had held me time and time
again and told me to
breathe.

hope's date with desolation

three streets down from town hall
there is a shopping cart stuck in the mud
across from the elementary school
whose swingset never fails to shriek.

who was so crass to roll these metal grates
a block away from the bustle of sunday shopping trips
bouncing over sidewalk cracks
tumbling into the wet spring dirt?

cheap metal is the ghost of the ditch.
its inhabitants rise from beneath,
attempting to weave through abandoned grates
desperately grasping at life beneath giants.

watch them reach towards the light.
watch them grow despite the intruder.

guiding lights

polaris met me in morrison, colorado
as my fingers purpled in 35° night.
she held my shaking hand as i traced the big dipper
across the wintry sky

cassiopeia hid behind denver's dome of skyglow
shielded her points from the tourists
in her absence, i remembered how it felt
to inhale frosty air beneath the milky way

that night i wanted nothing but the sun
as i could feel my toes frosting through two pairs of socks
a too-quiet night of shaky breaths and counting stars
searching for fornax and finding only the freeze

winter had come with a shock and a shiver
she left us with digits freezing in the dark
wondering how we had let the stars slip between our fingers
like sand.

get out of the mud!

good morning, blue eyes
i hadn't seen you sleeping there
but when you woke,
your gaze colored the sky to match the sea

you have risen amidst peonies and buttercups
and you are silent as you stir
as though afraid to waken
your sleeping petaled counterparts

summer is here;
whisper "sweet dreams" to the carnations
and bid them farewell
as the season ends

(and this year,
try not to fall asleep in the garden.)

stepping, stomping

the sun took my hand
and invited me on a stroll across the horizon.

i began to tiptoe along the rockies
but she taught me that it's sometimes okay to stomp
and that i can move the very mountains that hold up the sky.

we composed a skyline of footprints
until i learned how not to slide
until i wore denver's sunsets like a shawl.

i have found warmth in what's outside my window.
i still need to wear a sweatshirt when i step into the wind
but i know now to stand firmly
that it's okay to crack the ice
that i can make my own deep footprints
in this snowy groundcover.

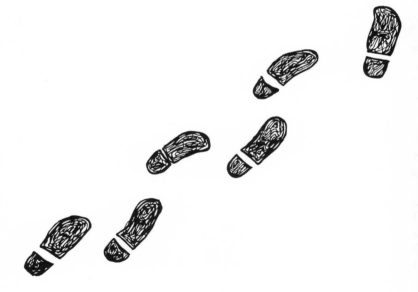

feathers hold poorly hammer and nails

i spent a couple of months building a nest, only to realize that i hadn't chosen the correct tree. sure, there's some appeal in construction: collecting branches and fallen leaves and abandoned pieces of yarn to create something of my own — but a nest isn't exactly secure if it's sitting in the dirt.

here's the thing about not having an obvious home: it becomes a lot more desirable to build one. is that sustainable? no. in fact, it's time consuming and a little expensive. but like a baby bird, i stood blind. i began to build before i figured out how to fly. i was fed one time and decided that i would build my home around that feeling — which was fine, until my stomach grew empty again and nobody answered my incessant, needy chirping.

i need to figure out how to use my beak for things besides building. i want to learn and to speak and to know how to get under rocks to eat grubs and stuff. god knows i need to work out how to fly. i'll never flap these wings if i'm too busy waiting for the next meal, or thinking about twigs and yarn. i'll never find the right branch if i can't get off the ground.

someone stomped on the nest i built, and now i'm standing in a pile of broken branches. the pieces are still there, but they aren't the same. it isn't what i dreamed of or worked hard at. this isn't what i wanted to build. and that's okay.

i can't survive sitting at the base of a tree; i need to find higher branches. not only that, i need to find the right tree, the right twigs, the right yarn. i can't settle down until i've seen every aspen, spruce, and maple. i can't go home until i've built it myself — the right way.

standing in this shitty, splintery mess of what once was, i can finally open these baby-bird eyes. there are others like me, pattering around on thin legs, talons getting stuck in the dirt. i can feel the air in these growing feathers. i know the wind will pick me up. i know i am not the only one still learning how to fly.

a poorly-timed meeting with time himself

i ran into father time on a monday,
practically body-checked him on a bustling
seattle street corner.
i felt the blood stop rushing through my veins
like the frozen cars in the street
like the sun paused mid-set in the sky
like the wind half-filtered through my hair.

he whispered to me
and i heard it clearly
thanks to the quieting of a billion clocks' murmurs.

he told me to cease my laments;
that no time was truly wasted.
like a pickpocket, he rifled through my wallet
and found that i'd been treating hours like currency.
went "tsk tsk tsk" and told me that seconds weren't a capitalist commodity,
not a common currency across that made-up dateline.
i was no richer for skipping the commercials.

he shut that leather wallet
and tucked it back into my jacket pocket.
soft skin stained by cigarette smoke,
he reeked of age but felt like youth.
he tapped me on the shoulder and that rush hour traffic
took to its roar again.

the world felt louder,
my wallet thinner,
my watch a little slower.

he had disappeared into seattle's stratus by the time i turned around.
i stood still as the traffic signals changed,
fiddling with the strap of my watch,
untying that analog calculator
from the skin of my wrist.

pebbles of conviction

the valley is shielded by the shadows of dawn
and its pious inhabitants greet the day from obscurity

the captain is always shrouded in light
his sermons sung by the winds
from 7000 feet

from their towers the cretaceous deities
wean their audiences off bibles and rosaries
until they know only cathedrals of stone

in their rejection of the pew
the zealots kneel on thank god ledge
in prayer

and yet they stand by
as their granite monoliths crumble
these seeming gods shielding their secularity
as they turn to sand.

state of the union

my right elbow aches
when it meets my bed
i've stopped sleeping and started
tossing and turning instead

i have some new calluses
and my skin has turned rough
i bumped my head and then wished
that my skull was more tough

the bruises on my thighs
purple me Long And Far
i picked at my shin's scab
and now it's a scar

i shredded my forearm
on a too-hard climb
my lungs complain when i
take the stairs two at a time

my hands are burning but these scratches won't stay
my bones shout profanities at me all day
my body is aching but i am okay
and no little injury
can take that away

cheap boots, drowned roots

her red rain boots are stuck in
march's mud and she knew
that it was pouring rain but
those droplets could hardly
interfere with the call of the garden
or the allure of growing
vegetables
and so she sloshed through
the fallen clouds
to see whether or not
her cucumbers were
blue-ribbon worthy
she did not consider
how little time had passed since
she last checked on her budding friends
and she had just bought herself
these nice red rain boots
rubber
shining with the promises of
successful yields and
years of use
but already she can feel the
cold of the wet dirt
through the thin material and
her mismatched multicolored socks
and she knows now that they were
overpriced
as the garden is being
swallowed by the storm
her plants
overrun by water
and she will not place at the county fair
and her red rain boots are ruined
and leaking
already.

babbling brook

i heard you speak over babbling brook
heard you mumble the wants of our mother
she begged me from my bootstraps
birthed me with imbalance so i would fall back into her

i watched that violent stream split two ways
and wanted to be held in the temporary arms of each.
why did you select this trail, with its roots and boulders?
did you not know how we would trip into her waters?
how these scraped knees would bleed into her skin?
how she would again call us home as our marrow
met ripple and riverbed?

she sent colder swells down the creek
and i couldn't help but jump in,
submerge myself in her watery bile,
and meet sleep before the river's fork.

spring cleaning

oh, hey, spring — sorry, it's a little messy in here
i haven't tidied up since september left
and locked the door behind her.

spring — oh, no, you don't have to do that!
i promise i'll get around to those dishes.
i've been trying to use less-toxic cleaners;
i hate it when the kitchen tile smells like bleach.

spring, could you open the shutters?
it's so nice to see the sun again.
if you want, you can sweep in the kitchen —
i'll be right back with the dustpan.

spring, you're so kind to help me with the chores.
there's a thin layer of grease coating the countertops —
what do you say we do something about that?
i'll make my bed as the dryer tumbles.

spring, your fingers smell like laundry detergent,
your hair like Febreze.
you feel like rebirth and familiarity.
the air tastes New in here.

spring, you're always a welcome house guest.
this time, i hope you'll stay awhile.

valley's monarch

looming she sat above the valley and did not mind
as the weekend's storm cascaded down her face
like tears after a long-term relationship
or a the rush of a stuck-on faucet

she turned forest ceilings to skylights
unavoidable prowled the sky
her armor shy,
gleaming only in the light of the moon

valiant and pensive was her rule
until she had captivated the minds of every artist that stood beneath her
until the valley became her kingdom

the trees bowed to her until their trunks arched
her vertical counterparts dared not outgrow her
mountains shrunk to boulders to avoid conflicts of size

they crowned her in jewels of granite
and upon a throne of rock she has remained since.

bruises

i've been nursing two bruised knees for months now.

i get scared clinging to icy rock so i Slam my patellas against
the stone until i feel in control again and
these desperate flings show themselves
in the purpling circles on my legs

i would like to issue a formal apology to my
ankles, whose cracked skin
is host to scratches that i won't let heal

i can't afford the luxury of taking a break and
waiting for my scabs to scar over,
so i hope that this momentum
heals all things

i rest my head between my abused knees
and feel the bumps of the freeway echoed in my skull

my body is wrapped safely in a seatbelt of
idle conversation and off-key singing
as i wait for my shoelaces to thaw.

symbiosis

my mother raised me to keep the mountains in my spine. sometimes the cascades escape from their capsules of vertebrae and adopt me into them instead. i never know when they'll come back, so i sleep on my side. i hold the planet beneath my forearm. its rivers and ridges flow over a down alternative. it snores and with those exhalations, the cherry blossoms bloom. feigning fall, those petals covered my rain-sticky driveway until a cruel winter razed the trees to their roots. i never wanted a picket fence. we let the rhododendrons grow and hid behind those lanceolate leaves instead. i'd get lost in those bushes until my mother called me home:

> "you'll   poke   your   eye   out !"

so be it. consider it an organ donation to this breathing entity, this matri-arch of oxygen, she who birthed carbon from her undersea exhalations. i wouldn't mind bleeding out in the backyard if it meant becoming fertiliz-er for her wildflowers.

the cascades always come home to me. sometimes, in my sleeping spoon, i feel them slip beneath my skin. i wake stiff and satisfied, my granite backbone returned from its affair with the horizon. i worry not of its loyalty. her spinning inertia moves from artery to vein. her mountains uphold my marrow. my spine upholds her sky.

ACKNOWLEDGEMENTS

The experience of making this book has been, in a word, terrifying. There's a lot more to it than I anticipated at the beginning: there's the hours of compiling and editing and designing, the loathing of every word you've ever written, the crushing anxiety that everyone you love will Hate the entire thing. It isn't exactly romantic. None of this would have happened without near-constant support and encouragement, and for that, I have a couple of people to thank.

Right off the bat, I can't thank Kimberly Kazanowski enough for her incredible work illustrating this book. I am absolutely blown away by her talent, and I feel so lucky that my words can be accompanied by her art.

To everyone who has read and edited and validated my poems – Andrew Korn, Alex Haworth, Maya Holt, Jenna Tseng – thank you for helping me see the value of my own words. You guys have given me just the right balance of support and criticism; I now enjoy my work, but like, not too much.

Sydney Lambert, Alisa Tvorun Dunn, Paige Grover, Kenna Kuhn, Alex Koon, Amy Harjes – thank you for your constant support and encouragement. I would never have pursued an actual self-motivated project if you guys didn't make me feel so valid every day. I'm so lucky to have so many supportive, brilliant women in my life!

Speaking of wonderful women: thank you to PJ Heusted (and our lizard son). You encourage (see: force) me to produce at least a little bit of content every month. Writing A Lizard Named Charlie with you has easily been the most rewarding experience of my life, and I am so proud of all we have created. You're the best co-author/partner in crime/friend I could ask for. (Say hi to Charlie for me!)

Finally, thank you to everyone else who has made my life so full. Stokers, Vertical World gang, Unglemoor Climbing Club: thank you for getting outside with me, because going outside is the only thing that keeps me sane. Most of the best experiences of my life have been in the outdoors, and they've been with you. I would not be the same person if I didn't love this planet as much as you all taught me to.

I've wanted to write ever since I learned how to read, so I cannot emphasize enough how much your love and support means to me. Whether you maybe kind of know me (or don't at all!) or you've edited my every word, your involvement with this book means the world to me. Thank you. :)

57332880R00047

Made in the USA
Middletown, DE
29 July 2019